Prepping on a Budget

Proper Management Is Key to Prepping

Prepping and Survival Series

Sneha Agrawal

Mendon Cottage Books

JD-Biz Publishing

Disclaimer

The information is this book is provided for informational purposes only. It is not intended to be used and medical advice or a substitute for proper medical treatment by a qualified health care provider. The information is believed to be accurate as presented based on research by the author.

The contents have not been evaluated by the U.S. Food and Drug Administration or any other Government or Health Organization and the contents in this book are not to be used to treat cure or prevent disease.

The author or publisher is not responsible for the use or safety of any diet, procedure or treatment mentioned in this book. The author or publisher is not responsible for errors or omissions that may exist.

Warning

The Book is for informational purposes only and before taking on any diet, treatment or medical procedure, it is recommended to consult with your primary health care provider.

Our books are available at

1. Amazon.com
2. Barnes and Noble
3. Itunes
4. Kobo
5. Smashwords
6. Google Play Books

Table of Contents

Introduction 4

Why is it so important to save food? 5

It is important to plan before storing 6

Allocation of money for storing food 7

Proper food management 8

Variety of food that can be stored 9

It is important to throw away decomposed food 13

Techniques of storing food for longer duration 14

Equipment and utilities that we need to have 16

Storage Techniques 19

Storage Methods 20

It is important to buy the correct products 22

Substitutes at the time of prolonged disaster 23

Water storage and its importance 25

Conclusion 26

Author bio 27

Publisher 37

Introduction

We are aware of the fact that disasters can strike at any time of day, and at any place. We are also aware of the fact that we should remain prepared to overcome any such situations and for that we should have some kind of backup.

We even know that we should always have some kind of food and water storage, for some days; this will ensure that we are able to live a normal life until the bad effect of the disaster is over. But, the whole question is do we actually follow the simple rule of life, or do we even know the whole process of prepping? Most of the time people face some kind of atrocious situation only because of lack of knowledge about a particular thing. This same case is applicable here, where one does not have adequate knowledge on what to store and how much to store. We sometimes waste a lot of money on buying what is not important and even if we buy correct supply, we do not have adequate knowledge about the storage system of food. This leads to wastage of lot of money, and also does not provide surety on the survival plan.

In this book we will discuss about all the parts in detail, so that a person is able to fight back in tough situations, without having to invest a lot of money in it.

Why is it so important to save food?

We stay in a world, which is under the threat of some kind of disaster, every single minute. Usually people do not have control over any kind of disaster, despite the fact; we should not give ourselves to the external situations.

We have a few basic necessities in life, without which it will be impossible to sustain in the world; food and water. When disaster strikes, availability of these two basic necessities gets jeopardized. One can have to face any kind of natural disaster like hurricane, heavy storm, blizzard, heavy winds and etc. or some manmade disasters; it also becomes tough to comprehend the number of days it will take for everything to go back to its normal state. At such times, it is very important to have a basic food supply stored in the house.

The local government and the rehabilitation team, goes at length, to provide help to all those people who are affected by a calamity, by providing them with food packets. However, the team does not provide the food packets on the basis of number of residents in a household; rather it follows a uniform supply policy for each household. This is one more reason for maintaining a proper food supply, for a few days, to combat any kind of disaster.

It is important to plan before storing

There are a few factors which we need to know before we could start storing food as per the contingency plan. At first we need to determine the number of permanent members of our house and their special requirements, if any. For example, if we have a diabetic patient staying with us, or an infant we need to take care off, they are supposed to follow a specific kind of dietary plan and we need to store the food accordingly.

We also need to look around the place we stay in and determine the availability of free space, which can make use of, for proper storage of food. It must not happen that we waste our money in providing food for rodents!

Before storing the food, we should be well versed with the geographical location and its factors. For example, if we stay in a hilly area then our food storage plans will be different as compared to when staying at some beach area.

There is one more thing to remember and that one is supposed to keep food that has good shelf life even without a refrigerator, and can be cooked without much of a heat. We will also keep in account that water might not be available at the time of a disaster strike, so we should store food that require less water for preparation. It is advised to store food that is light and easy to carry because one might have to relocate for some time, and carrying bulky food might not be a good idea.

Allocation of money for storing food

It is important to understand the importance of storing proper food and water, to combat any kind of disastrous situation. We will need to spare some money, so that we can get together a prepping plan on budget. It is not necessary to store heavy price food items for disaster, but the normal food products itself. If you can have regular food even at the time of disaster then you will feel at home, and will be able to calm your mind. However, you will need to dispense some money in storing the food, which you can do over a period of a few weeks. It is not important that you store all the food at once and spend all your savings on it.

Let us take one example to understand it better. Hypothetically, let us assume that you use one liter of olive oil in a month, and then just before the month ends, you put olive oil in the purchase list during your next visit to grocery store. Now, this time you are supposed to buy two bottles of olive oil in the list and as soon as one bottle is consumed, buy one more bottle again. This will ensure that you always have a bottle of olive oil extra in your store. When you allocate your budget in this way, then you will not even feel the pressure of the budget and you will be able to manage any kind of situation successfully.

Proper food management

Disasters do not happen often, but it takes a continuous preparation to combat any kind of disaster. It is not only necessary to store food and water for contingencies, but it is also very important to manage them properly. We need to keep replenishing our food stock, with the latest manufactured ones, and need to use the old stock. One should not just throw away the stocked food item, because they could not be used during some disaster. We should always keep looking at the expiry dates mentioned in the stored food items and consume them when they start getting old. We do not store any special kind of food for our disaster management plan, but we store daily routine food items, so we can use them even on a daily basis. This proper management of food will also help us manage our scarce funds diligently.

Different kinds of food items are required to be replenished at various time intervals; however we should aim to clear off all the old stock within a month or two. For the packed food items that have an expiry time of one-two years, they should be replenished within every six months. At the time of a disaster strike, one must always try and get the latest food stock from a local vendor, because one can never predict the duration of the disaster nor its normalizing time.

Variety of food that can be stored

It is important to understand that one cannot get choosy in storing the eatables for emergencies. You cannot compromise on the quantity of food for taste, at the time of emergency situations. It is important to store the food which will not get putrid, in a short duration. We will also need to understand that during an emergency, even availability of water becomes scarce, so we will need to store food which does not demand consuming lot of water, post eating. Examples of food that need to be avoided are fat rich food, oily and spicy food and etc.

Apples

When apples are stored in a dry and cool place, away from early ripening fruits like bananas, they can last for 2-3 months. They have enough minerals and vitamins, which can take care of nutrition requirement for months.

Citrus fruits

A few citrus fruits like oranges and grapefruits have vitamin C in them which keeps the body hydrated. This is one reason that food storage plans should have some kind of citrus fruits in it. Moreover, if they are purchased in a non-ripened state, then they can last for 2-3 weeks, without refrigerators. When there is scarcity of water, one can have citrus fruits to keep a proper water balance in the body.

Potatoes

Potatoes can be used to make delicious side dishes, along with the mains, at the time of a disaster strike. Potatoes can last for more than a month, when stored in cool and dark area. They are also a great source of energy, and during the time of contingency they can prove to be a great energy source.

Raw food

It is not always necessary that one will have access to cooking gas or a cooling medium at the time of disaster, so it is important to keep some food stock that can be eaten raw. A typical example of such an item is cucumber, which can last for some days, without refrigeration.

Grains and Bread

They are the dry food items that come in packed cartons, which can be supportive for more than 3 months, when stored in room temperature.

Butter/Oil

Butter contains healthy fats which is important for the body to maintain a proper energy level and other body systems. They can be stored without any refrigeration and have a long shelf life. Dietary oil like olive oil is good for your health and has about two years of shelf life. They however, carry huge cost and thus one needs to store in less quantity of olive oil.

Spices and Herbs

Food becomes tasteless when they are supposed to be eaten raw, without any spices sprinkled on them. Even at the time of a disaster strike, you are not supposed to eat tasteless food. One can store small quantities of natural herbs like thyme, rosemary, etc., and also some spices like red pepper. There are times when stored spices come in very handy, for example, at the time of extreme cold. One can make spicy soup, at such times, which will help in keeping your body system warm.

Wheat berries

It is always advised to store wheat berries instead of flour, for emergency purpose. Flour has a shelf life of a few months whereas wheat berries has a shelf life of years.

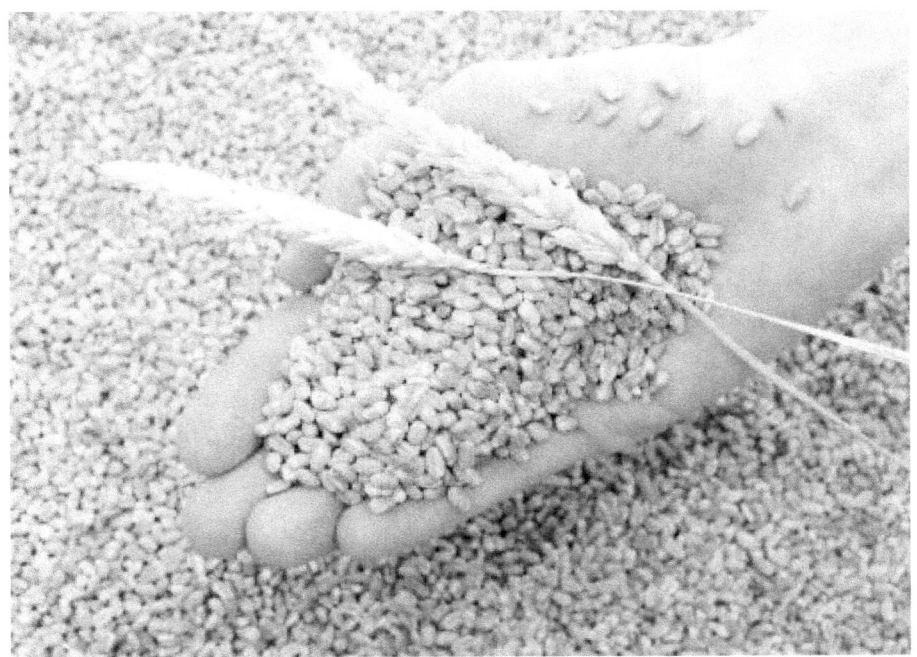

Wheat berries ready for grinding

Canned food and Dry Mixes

Nowadays prepping on a budget has become easier with the invention of canned and packed food items. They come in ready to eat form and can be stored for more than 6 months' time. A few typical examples are corn flakes, cup noodles, energy bars and etc.

Baby milk substitutes and Baby food

This section of product is limited only to those households that have a small baby to take care of. Infants and babies do not eat much variety and thus it is important to maintain a proper food supply for them, even if it means wastage of some money. When adults are hungry then they can sustain on any kind of food or even some time without food, but it is not same with babies. We get milk powders in packed containers, which are made especially for babies, and have long shelf life. We should store them adequately.

Ready-to-eat packets

It is always a good habit to store in some ready-to-eat food packets like pasta, frozen pizza, noodles and etc. They can be prepared instantly at the time of crisis with no great technical help, and can be rotated very easily on a daily basis.

Other necessities

There are other daily necessities like salt, sugar, tea bags and etc. which are to be stored in adequate quantity as they have a shelf life of 100 years. Rather than storing coffee powder it is always advised to store coffee beans as they have greater shelf life. We can make use of a wheat berry grinder to grind the coffee beans.

Here is a very useful link about food storage.

https://www.lds.org/topics/food-storage?lang=eng

It is important to throw away decomposed food

In order to save some cents, one should not compromise on the quality of the food. If you find that a particular food does not smell good then it is best to discard that food immediately. If you had to face a storm, then it is advised that you throw away all the food which came in contact with the storm water.

If we do not throw away the food item that has already rotted, then it will damage other products as well. Throw all the canned food items that are bulging and remained opened for a longer duration of time. You will also need to take care of the dairy products and meat, because they are damaged within 2-3 days.

Before moving further to storage techniques, it is important to get a brief on what factors work behind the deterioration of food. There are a few natural factors as well as external factors that destroy our food. Enzymes are one natural factor that spoils the food, and are naturally present in food. With time, they start showing effect on food, especially on vegetables and fruits. External factors include bacteria and rodents. Now, there are certain bacteria which grow only when there is ample amount of oxygen present, but some grow even without oxygen. If we find that the food smells bad then we should just throw them out as they might be infected by severely harmful bacteria.

We however, can save the food from rodents like rats, by maintaining a proper storage system in house. Rodents eat up some food and spoil the rest, so their entry should be restricted at any cost.

Techniques of storing food for longer duration

As mentioned earlier, there are few factors which work behind spoiling of food. Basically there are two ways of which we can minimize the effects of such factors.

Drying or dehydrating food

The main reason for any food item to get spoiled is the moisture content in it. Without the presence of moisture, harmful bacteria will not be able to thrive and will not damage the food. Even the enzymes which work behind the decaying of food become inactive, with the absence of moisture. When dry food items are kept in air tight containers, which prevent moisture from getting inside the jars, the food item will sustain for a longer duration.

The best way to store such food items is by keeping them out in sun, if possible, for some time. Because of dehydration, the food item gets lighter and compact, which also facilitates their proper storage.

Dehydrated fruits.

Freezing

Freezing again is a good technique for storing food for a longer time period. This method however, is applicable only at times when there is a continuous supply of electricity. Even if there is no supply of electricity, one can make use of a fuel generated freezer. When food is stored in very cold temperatures then enzymes do not work on food and even harmful bacteria are not able to thrive in intense cold temperatures.

One can store dairy products, meat and etc. in a freezer, but ensure that they are consumed in the starting days of a disaster strike, as they decompose in a very short time span.

Equipment and utilities that we need to have

It is not always necessary that at the time of disaster strike we are able to access the gas line or that we have an adequate supply of electricity. For example, at the time of a heavy storm and lightning strike, our whole electrical set up may be damaged and we might not get access to electricity for a few days altogether. In such cases we must not depend only upon the ready-to-use food or raw food products. We should have some other backup to cook food. We can make use of various other natural resources to cook the food.

At first, it is important to keep a hand grinder at home, which can be used to grind grains like wheat berries. The hand grinders are age old equipment, which were used before industrialization. It will not hurt much to invest in such grinders for once. They are easy to use and do not take a lot of space for storing.

There are some disasters that are not related to weather changes, a typical example would be a chemical blast. In such cases the power or gas supply is stopped for some time, but still we can make use of the solar energy, which is available in abundance. We can harness the solar energy through solar cookers, and use them to cook food. The solar cookers are a bit overpriced, but they are a one-time investment. The people in places which receive good amounts of sunlight should consider buying solar cookers for an emergency time.

Even if you are able to utilize the hand grinder properly, you will still need something for actually cooking your bread. Charcoal ovens and grillers come in very handy at such times. They work on charcoal and are readily available in most stores. One can even grill chicken, cottage cheese, raw vegetables and other eatables in this griller. One can even make use of ovens to bake the bread. We can even make use of a camp stove which runs on natural fuel and will be very useful at the time when there is no electricity supply at your place.

Charcoal grill.

There are other small requirements that we need to take care of like an adequate amount of natural fuel like charcoal, kerosene, and etc. They are one time investment products and can be stored easily, and when safety is concerned, we should be ready to do that kind of investment. We however, need to take proper care while storing them. Fuel should not be stored in an inflammable zone otherwise they will catch fire and become a cause of disaster. Charcoal should be saved from a moist environment otherwise it will not be of any use at the time of an emergency.

There are other things like paper plates, cups and glasses, which should be stored in adequate amount because at the time of disaster we may not have access to adequate water supply and washing regular utensils, will become a big problem.

Storage Techniques

We store canned food, carton packed food and others for our emergency needs, and also we use them on a daily basis. Usually we store them on wooden or metal racks, on top of one another. We should take care of one fact that we store the latest purchase at the back of a stack. This process will ensure that we use the prior purchased food on a daily basis and we store the latest one for emergency purposes. This will also ensure that we do not waste our money just because of lack of proper food management.

We should also take care of one fact that we store the food at such a place which can be accessed easily, because you never know what lies in the future and how much time you have to grab the essentials. It may happen that despite storing all the food items, you are not able to reach them in time and they do not provide much of a help. Very essential food products like biscuits, energy bars and etc. should be kept in such a way that they are easily accessible even to kids. When it is about disaster management and prepping, one should remain prepared to combat any kind of tough situation.

It is also important to have a mix of different sized containers for storing food and label each container with the food name on them. Usually we miss on such small details, but they trouble us a lot at the time of an emergency. If we plan and manage properly then we can even save on the money deposited on such containers. We can buy packs of them, and get good offers. One thing noteworthy here is that, a container should be bought from a good brand as they are made of plastic. If we get bad plastic then even that will hamper the nutritional value of the food that we store in containers.

Storage Methods

It is not only enough to collect the right kind of food but it is also more important to store them properly so that they do not spoil. We store a multitude of food, with different shelf lives. There are a few which are vulnerable to small weather changes and some do not get rotten easily. Since, the food we store have different characteristics, we need to apply various methods to save a variety of food.

In- ground storage

We have a very natural storage medium that is readily available to us and that is in-ground storage. We can actually store certain root vegetables at our backyards, for some time. There are certain root vegetables, like carrot, parsnips, turnips and etc. which can be dumped into the ground and covered with dry leaves or straw. Best time to follow the above mentioned method is winter time, when the root vegetables will remain fresh for some time. They can be retrieved back and when required the crop will sustain for some weeks to come. We can even store leafy crops like lettuce, and cabbage via this method.

Root-cellars

There were days when people used to specially make root cellars in their houses to keep fruits and root vegetables fresh. A root cellar is nothing but a small room made in a basement area, which generally remains very cool. Fruits and root vegetables require some moisture and cool temperature to remain fresh and a root cellar fulfills the requirements perfectly.

Metal racks

We can place open or closed metal racks at a corner of our kitchen. It does not occupy lot of space and is also very cost-effective. We can store all the packed containers, packets, and cartons on this rack, one on top of another. We can even save our food by placing rat kill around the rack, and storing rodent prone food on top shelves. Racks can be made out of wood also but again they are prone to moisture and might also damage the stored food.

Metal shelves to store food.

Air tight containers

We have learned in earlier chapters that food spoils because of excessive moisture content present in air. We should store grains, pulses, and other items in air tight containers, so that they do not deteriorate with time.

Dry Ice

Dry ice is nothing but CO_2 gas in solid form, which keeps our refrigerator cool. They can last for a few days if stored in cool place, and they evaporate with time. This is a very temporary set up for certain situations like power failure for few days. If we get to know that there will be major power cut for few days altogether, then we can store some dry ice in our freezer and keep the freezer running. All the food items stored in freezer will not spoil because of a power cut.

It is important to buy the correct products

We should always be careful about the manufacture and expiry date mentioned in that food packet, when we buy them from stores. Usually the store owners try to push old products, but it is our own duty to buy what is best for us. One should make it a habit to check the dates, and then only go for buying.

It is a healthy practice to check for the constituents mentioned in the pack and then go for the buying of a product. The constituents will let us know whether we are buying healthy stuff or not. If we buy something that putrefies easily then we will not be able to store that for a long time.

We have often witnessed that there are many companies that provide huge discounts on bulk purchases and even we fall prey to the promotional techniques. For example, we can avail huge discounts on milk cartons when bought in bulk. Now, we need to understand that if we face some disaster and there is no power supply then that full carton will go to waste without any cool storage medium. So, we should always invest our money on buying diligently.

If we find that a particular carton has been tampered with, then we should avoid buying such items, even if we get good discounts on them. They might harm us severely, so it is important to ensure that whatever we bring is sealed properly.

Substitutes at the time of prolonged disaster

Disasters strike without any prior notice and similarly nobody can predict about the duration of the disaster. It may happen that without even your noticing it, disaster will strike and its effects will be lost within some time. For such times, all the above mentioned techniques will be quite helpful for managing your daily food requirements. However, there are disasters like nuclear radiation and heavy storms which do not leave their mark soon. They make people suffer for a prolonged period and usually we run out of our food stock, when the disaster strike goes on for such a long period. For such times it is important that you should know some techniques to grow your own food. This may sound a bit unusual, but creating your own food supply is the best chance for surviving such disastrous times. It is not necessary that we grow each and every kind of food that we eat, but we should be in a position to grow basic vegetables and cook bread for ourselves.

Growing vegetables

Most of the houses have a backyard which can be used to grow some vegetables, at the time of disaster. It takes time for crop to grow, so if we get an early indication that the conditions will not normalize soon, we should start thinking of planting vegetables in our backyard. The process of growing vegetables in your backyard is simple and does not involve complex training. It can be learned through a book or even by articles published on the internet. One must however, remain prepared to carry on this job as well, and store all pre-requisites for the process.

Fishing and Hunting

Fishing and hunting are age old practices to maintain a proper food supply at the time of a disaster strike. However, fishing and hunting may not be possible, especially if we stay in the city which is situated far away from a pond and forest area. Nevertheless, if we have an option of fishing then we must definitely explore it. We should know the basics of fishing and hunting so that we can support ourselves at the time of disaster strike.

Raise your own livestock

It is not in purview of everyone to raise an animal for his daily needs, but if the need should arise one must be prepared to breed animals like chickens and such. Chickens can become a great source of daily egg supply, and sometimes can even provide us with meat. It is always good to have some background knowledge on breeding chickens, which will be helpful at the time of an emergency. When you get to know about the disaster strike, what best you can do is get the pre-requisites of breeding a hen. It might turn out to be the best decision taken at the time of disaster.

Form social groups and maintain supply

When the disaster strikes for a prolonged period it usually becomes impossible to survive alone. Imagine a situation wherein there is no source of entertainment; no television, internet or laptops. There seems to be just one way of surviving and that is by forming one large group of people staying in a single locality. All the people would have stored something or other for emergency needs; clubbing all the food resources and the skills of people, you can support each other at the time of disaster. Some would know the process of grinding wheat berries and some would know the process of baking bread out of it. Clubbing all the efforts of different people, and following the age old barter system, will be easy to sustain in worst times.

Water storage and its importance

When we are talking about budget prepping for food supply it is important to throw some light on the prepping methods of proper water supply at the time of disaster. One thing worth mentioning in here is that a person can survive without food for a few weeks, but surviving without water is impossible even for a few days. Typically we need about one gallon of water on a per day basis, per person. We will dehydrate because of lack of water and will not survive longer, if there is no adequate supply of water.

The most basic fact that every person needs to remember is that the water supply gets extinct before the food supply, and thus as soon as there is announcement of any kind of disaster strike, it is important to store an adequate amount of water in tanks and containers. We will need water for drinking purposes as well as for other necessities. We need to store some fresh water for drinking and water for other necessities.

Apart from storing an adequate amount of water it is also important to store some disinfectant tablets so that they can be made use of in emergency needs. There are sources like ponds and lakes which can serve as a source of fresh water, but they will need to be purified with the help of disinfectant tablets.

When disaster strikes then usually it has a ripple effect, and one kind of damage will lead to another. It is important that we do not let this happen and maintain disinfected water supply. We should always use purified water especially if we have an infant to take care of, at the time of a disaster strike.

Conclusion

We cannot stop disasters from happening but we can definitely prepare ourselves for facing the worst. Food and water are two of the most basic necessities that we will need for survival, and thus taking a special care of food and water supply is must. Though, it is not advisable to store unnecessary food, because it will cost us money. It is important to manage the stored food and keep them rotating properly on a daily basis. If you can manage your food supplies properly then it will ensure that without much blocking of money you will be able to store a month's supply easily.

As discussed, it is not only important to store food but to also be prepared to go one step ahead. You should be prepared to cultivate your own food and breed your own livestock, so that you are able to sustain for a prolonged period of disaster. You should also be prepared to club with other people around and sustain as a whole society.

Apart from food, you will also need to take care of your water supply, especially your daily water intake. If you can store water properly, half of your problems will be taken care of. With proper management, there is no problem that cannot be tackled, even if is managing disastrous situations.

Author bio

Books are a great medium of sharing one's own experiences with the outer world, and enhancing the knowledge of the readers. With this same purpose, I, Sneha Agrawal share this write-up with my readers.

I am an MBA graduate from a top notch Business School of India, and have done specialization in marketing and finance stream. I also hold some work experience as a team leader, for one of the known Indian IT companies.

To live a successful life, one should always have the answers of a few questions, at any point in time and they are what, how and when; and I live my life in search of these answers.

Our books are available at

1. Amazon.com
2. Barnes and Noble
3. Itunes
4. Kobo
5. Smashwords
6. Google Play Books

Check out some of the other JD-Biz Publishing books

Gardening Series on Amazon

Country Life Books

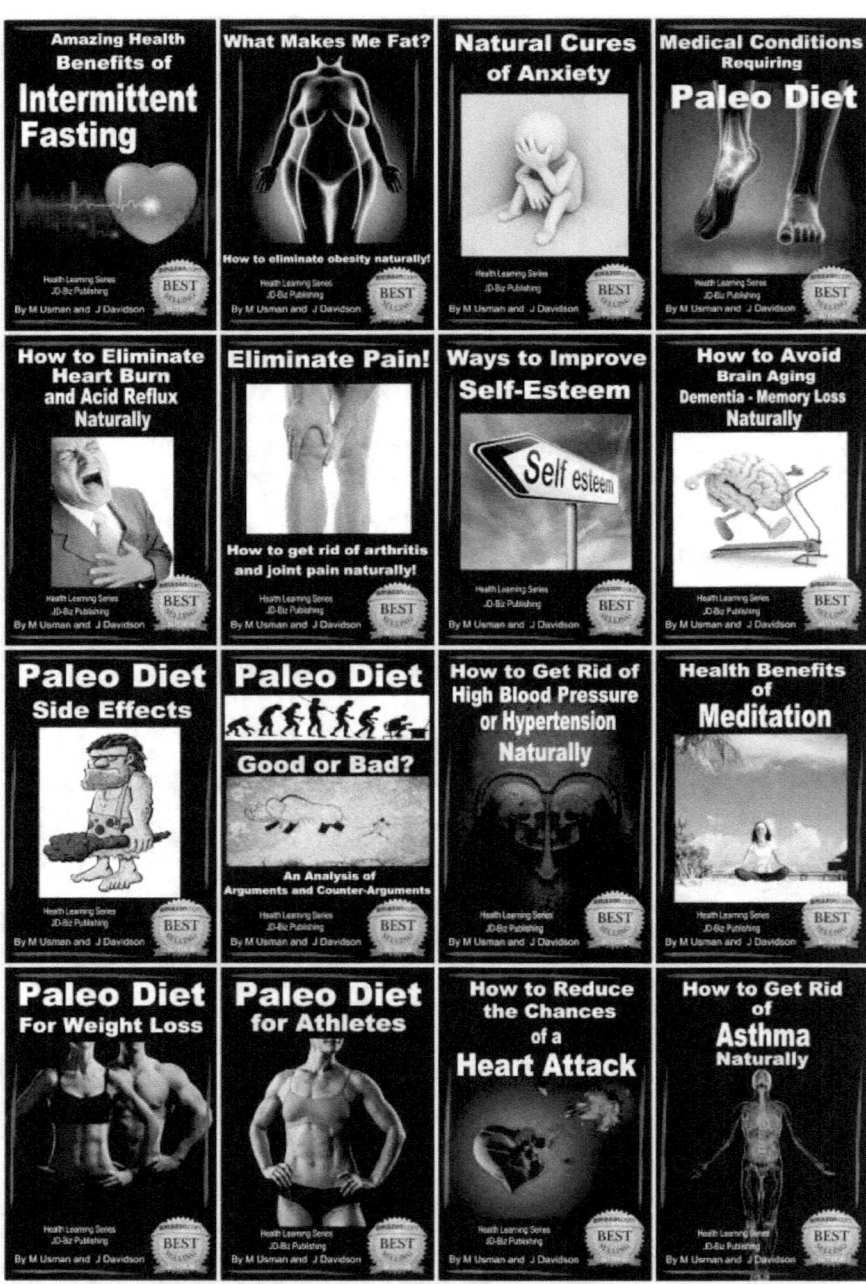

Learn To Draw Series

How to Build and Plan Books

Entrepreneur Book Series

Publisher

JD-Biz Corp

P O Box 374

Mendon, Utah 84325

http://www.jd-biz.com/

Mendon Cottage Books

P O Box 374, Mendon Utah 84325

www.ingramcontent.com/pod-product-compliance
Lightning Source LLC
Chambersburg PA
CBHW061936280526
45787CB00004B/1624